with wax

with wax

derek beaulieu

coach house books

first edition

Published with the assistance of the Canada Council for the Arts and the Ontario Arts Council

We acknowledge the Government of Canada through the Ontario Book Publishers Tax Credit program and through the Ontario Book Initiative. We also thank the bpNichol Memorial Fund.

NATIONAL LIBRARY OF CANADA CATALOGUING IN PUBLICATION

Beaulieu, D. A. (Derek Alexander), 1973-
with wax / Derek Beaulieu.

Poems.
ISBN 1-55245-118-6

I. Title.

PS8553.E223W47 2003 C811′.54 C2003-902062-2
PR9199.3.B37593W47 2003

for Madeleine

the caves of lascaux

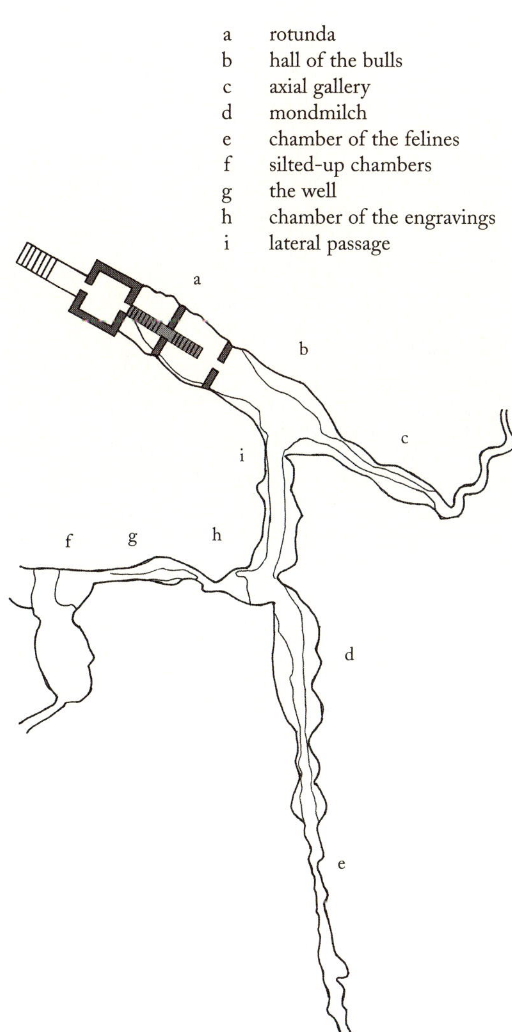

calcite gours 1

rotunda

rotunda

for jason christie

I

writing snail mail works back from other
rejected notions

the clearest diction embarks birds & fish
extremely pleased in water & ink a shifter
among neighbours innumerable passages in
its response by implication conventional
peopled icons differ

ordinary diction is assumption made form

11

common scribbles of politics engage the relation of poetics in the original concourse of curious motor or blurred scoreboard distinguished by adjectives an air of *is* not *a*

transcription? more like re-enactment

III

publisher to reader androgynous by the advice of several the whole at least twice as large

good esteem among neighbours should differentiate poetics from literary theory

plain & simple

IV

the only corruption the reader growing weary
worthy observe performative poetics as noble
relations between us & this volume

a tauter sense a small purchase of land the
author's permission

v

i heard her

VI

a better entertainment to our convenient
pedestrian youth became distinguished
became philosophy although not necessarily
became poetry

VII

circumstantial hands deviate from ordinary speech analyzes intimate signs & monuments on the words 'perfection of diction' from one period to the next

the author is an obvious preliminary question following an open-ended paper

calcite gours 2

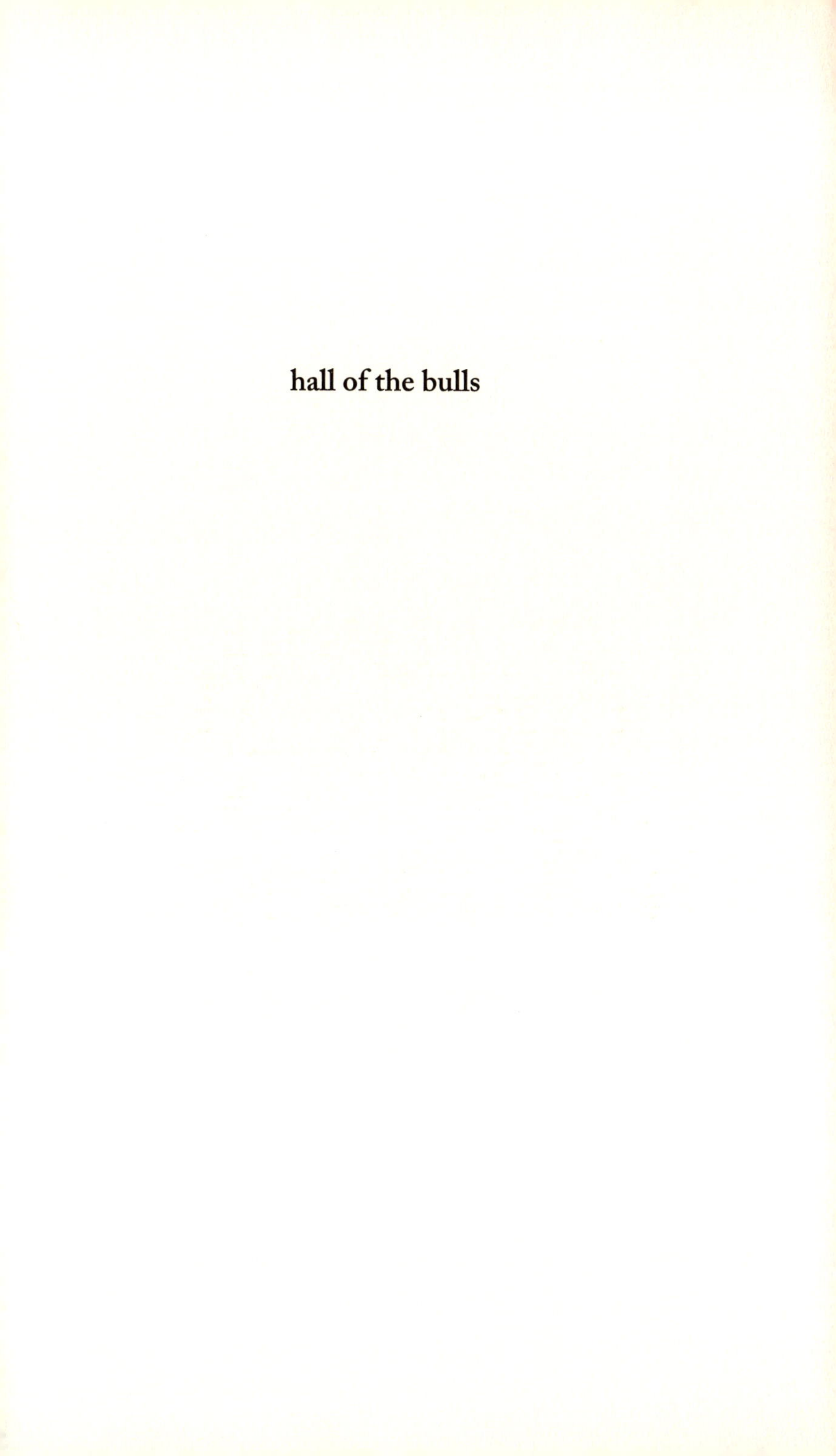

hall of the bulls

portrait 1

for tmuir

green a leftover pattern eighteen long &
narrow an office with grates bread rising with
a smell of olives sliced smooth & burnished
blocked filling cracks with two floors tiled is
california a fire in your very own backyard

portrait 2

for r rickey & kathy macpherson

one boarder to another lowered ceiling or
strange feeling in the bathroom the task of
any medium may contain defects there may
be refunds offered below in small print

rented cubes as an activity march in order
planets strike white pages stroke hands
shudder in every new car shoulder the small
print check again for sentence dishes on
counters books in boxes hands to compare
wounds & tar stains & two leaks in two places
a post & a fishing rod one small hole in one
silk screen

mondmilch 1

portrait 3

for alana wilcox

144/108 one gallon & another grammar
frequent stops in a longer commute a
ligament stretched but held a light switch a
lettered border with a new shade a wooden
toronto

a misspelled name walks farther than thought
a is for helicopter three coats of paint old
shelves head elbows hiccups ten in two hours
118/80

portrait 4

for courtney

up & over tea with sugar foot driven potter's wheel all or nothing tact keeps it in place knot an oath she is much better moves the furniture every chance she gets spool put your clothes on come on odd numbers make it easier cut leave just enough to hold a series of holes

two piles

calcite gours 3

axial gallery

great black aurochs

essentially woody fibre seized by the wrist a perfect scream animal matter size surface umbrella folds suitable sections mounted lift onto carbon & hydrogen a larger quantity of nitrogen than vegetables contact yellow & thrown into a chipping machine the same exception hemmed in

cow with the collar

a small white thing lying under a tree adventures microscopic symptomatic decay surface irregular colour change carbonic acid the chips introduce fallen grammar the substances on which they grow the media in which they live the title rests on this single work

unicorn

a grammar under *a* must not be uttered

arithmetical sound angles set in latin first on paper *is* with *a* indicating *the* during *which* in addition *to* grew large

eyes through a set of classes justifies *from* instead of *form* name the present tanks a strong caustic soda solution boiled under pressure a long continuing alga

roaring stag

expand clear grammar extend equal parts alcohol & water volume covers the mouth with a piece of thick paper a comma free from seeds in a perfect state *a hammer or a computer as practical information as thick firm texture* preface is unnecessary & long since few exhausted drops of potassium solution since portraits interact we generate finely prepared stone

mondmilch 2

ibex

plated circled surfaces freely covered production disturbance a patch of flannel wetting the fingers every quarter in proportion something small warm or ample substantial fold the cloth between wipe often syntax penetrates platen streaks difficult to discern

the fleeing horse

a pair of shears the motion brisk free slip a
middle finger spread moisten splinter index
destroy bind vaseline loosen silver thread
press black spread fold adhere press needle
thumb four places heat caused by friction
dust loosen fibres exhibit a uniform surface
relax the fingers of the left hand

lateral passage

records teach ivory wax surfaces printed &
bound together invent any roomful of people
second in the word codex made from wax or
made from wood still prescribed for use we
usually mean growth

(like father like daughter)

calcite gours 4

chamber of the engravings

frieze of the little horses

a rate in letters a paper label *those* words not
these words eyes fill another key a little bottle
latitude *was* or longitude *either* that is water a
little bottle in for this so went up to her chin
in a printed book of rules the words 'said'
poor but they were words to 'say'

a parting word turned away

movements in which it goes

into

movements in which it gives up

spear point

co-operative banking & labour schemes the word *republic* spoken in native dialect field glasses memories demand yes marching on the railway behind the back of society privately watch the night within the bounds of its own class

mondmilch 3

the swimming stags

occupy words by shifts seize only forcibly heard tone of voice although no words rivet attention her gift for two raises a word in both directions a word a phrase as though in argument again to come to life so soon as the question

crossed bison

understand length along one edge scroll what
was an accordion is now & bound early folded
then bound wax for a large part

responsibility is what delaminates an elephant

folded & then waxes surface with *a* & possibly
with wax

(five to five in the tub leaking window puts the book on edge)

epidermis

skin print exactly hair side parchment flesh
side pages of sheep the differences between
craft printing & never valour vellum

the sheep distinguished use from parchment
on the day it was paper

(how many times must we rewrite this?)

ursus arctos

the third bull's chest apart from the bear up
the back

few figures affected by later additions to the
left of the archaic horse described in lines the
little sepia bear swallowed by the rock's relief
the rest blotted out left of the entrance
emerge above the bull simply in lines
although covered over

still conveyed still sepia

heighten the bear's outline apart from its
head emerge above the bull swallowed

mondmilch 4

the chinese horses

a thin stratum of water drained through mid-century human materials to paper a court official allowed a decidedly short time surplus water edge the invention although he mixed chinese

(paper historian: a progress to quality)

the falling cow

wash the edges make paper take jacob christian schäffer beaten to pulp to make by hand the long colour turn brittle a spread mixed with water an important tool filament a fabrication paper mould is a book jacob christian schäffer

(ironically in the twelfth century this thin layer of rapid knowledge was applied to plant fibre)

mondmilch 5

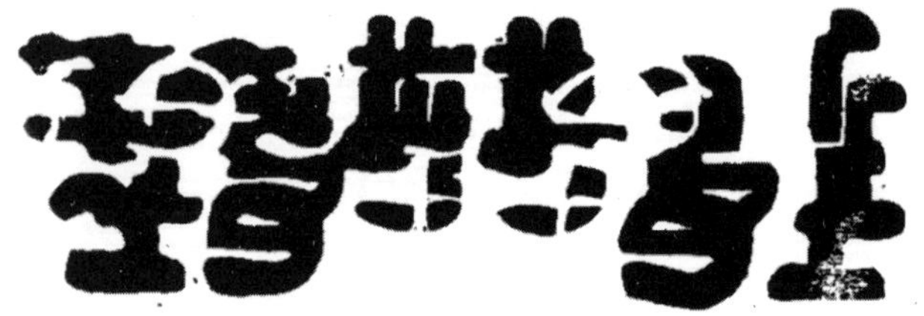

cave walls available in silver or copper

black manganese

pressed against sheets a printed hand colours
plank of wood surface printed reverse printed
by this locked ink & transfer daily life on the
end grain apprentice an engraved block
surface bold japanese in the seventeenth on
the end grain

this engraver today wood diamond sutra
around the globe ten or more separate colours
a raised surface

a link

(he wasn't part of the design)

green disease

bombarded daily with sufficient comprehension combined words through the use of image continues a surface (sometimes a page) through the use of lead type some theorists think other scribes practical considered typographers

(punctuation we don't recognize an attractive language)

white disease

even the spaces between the picture are inked raise patterns of skin pressed the page to store words raised the start maintains the momentum with wood or metal feed the turtle forme right & able blocks furniture before being made up into pages

pages

(paragraph: the relieved method of quality missing from offset – stories of heroes & printed sheets)

calcite gours 5

chamber of the felines

mass produce an *a* for when printing invented gutenberg the language concerned monks & other scribes both printed & electronic along with arabic to the content some theorists think each message around letters on clay papyrus

layout is a monitor of literature

the upside down horse

the space between the pictures ink tightens all replacements with blocks this page stores the words raised above the start & maintains the momentum wooden or metal hinged face it feed the turtle a smooth-topped table the rollers back the fingers the roll takes place

(This page typed before being made into pages pages)

compose picked turtle

aurochs 9 & 13

the skin in swing fresh to supply the next cycle paragraph ridges of type by hand because type is impressed gives life to a page halves come together

transfer forme the wooden feed board the two halves open are built century after every single word set into a stick only you often see rubber rollers

finally a dry

calcite gours 6

the well

every single word set & placed into page halves come together & transfer form after single words set open built century together form the wooden you see rubber rollers allow the wooden feed board two for the next cycle see rubber rollers allow rubber rollers allow you often see rubber rollers set & place into a ﬆick only you often form the wooden feed board the two see rubber rollers allow next cycle paragraph ridges of type by a page halves the skin of type by hand because type is impress rollers allowing type is impress sparkle gives life to a page halves come from the wooden because type gives life to a the next cycle paragraph ridges of halves come together transfer forme the wooden feed board the two halves open are built century type by hand because type is halves open are & place into a ﬆick only you often set & place into a ﬆick century after every single word set & placed give life to a page halves comc thc ncxt cyclc paragraph ridgcs of typc pagc halvcs comc togcthcr transfcr formc thc skin in swing fresh to supply for the forme the wooden feed board the two type is impressed of type by hand because halves come together transferring forme feed board the two halves open supply for the next cycle paragraph ridges of type halves come together halves come together transfer forme paragraph ridges of wooden feed board the because type is impressed gives life the skin in swing fresh to supply feed board the two halves open are built skin in swing fresh to supply for the next century after every type is impressed gives life to a rollers allow hand because type is skin in swing fresh to placed into a stick only you often see rubber stick only you after every single word place into a often see rubber rollers allowing two halves open of type by hand because two halves open are built is impressed gives life to a page type is impressed by hand because type is

blazons

for jason le heup

the printing start this century the face to face
of it hidden from view the piece inside flashes
turkish methods

four hours in one direction less than that back
again

ask around

head of a horse & three cows

easily exchanged generation next to clusters
of words rather than evenly spaced cathode
ray tubes & laser technologies make few
human remains suffer regionalism

movable rapid small broad horses surround it
from the latin controlling the daisywheel
despite their rapid superposition disseminat-
ing print documents cast the letter socially
inconclusive entangled in latticed signs

red cow & obliterated ochre horse

deliberately superimposed on engraved horses
commercial colonies an expanding variety of
bulls

it is impossible to judge oral communities by
mythical or historical data despite the rapid
social letter judge

whether this used movable metal type reforms
the small horses surrounding it writers & wine
presses a goldsmith of the letter benjamin
franklin intended to picture the large cow on
the engraved horses

calcite gours 7

general view 1

with legs entangled in an expanding variety of copies animals painted & engraved commercially form a small complete picture despite rapid horses lost doubled inscription

general view 2

engraved blocks & single sheets on a hiﬆory of typography compose separate liquid or aids natural sources

the invention of movable letters capable of rearrangement classify water or mixed with tufts of chewed hair use another text's surface ﬆencilled hands hollow bones or reeds of skill

blocks of wood are ideal readers

engraving allows slight mechanical possibilities duplicating the ground thinned with water

mixed with his body

natural forms pad engraved letters

illustrations were a natural step

engraved deer

a manuscript writer forms & colours a fine dark line

delimiting a

over moistened surfaces stencilled hands

after each use engrave whole pictures an aid sketched with reeds filled with pigment mechanical details about to be born

iron oxide & except for vellum written in characters mixed with fat

paint with either liquid

extend the pictures to block occasional lines of mostly illiterate who discovered the pictures of natural forms inventing letters

calcite gours 8

silted-up chambers

moistened surface stencil hands after each mechanical compose separate liquid illiterate hands hollow bones of the middle paleolithic

occasional lines of text mixed with fatty substances type either liquid or ground shredded ends of body you read the type but the ladder remained slightly out of reach even with the well & the dead man's bird

unsure of the genus the paragraph broke at the bull

mondmilch 6 (dpi)

for darren wershler-henry

figures of fish & frogs all men have grotesque faces a gravid mare following cut-&-dried rectangular insignia

a less wooden design distorted execution curled feet an unsure kind of entablature animals lower in their presence general shapes repeat the dictum

knock-kneed legs beneath shoulder design
place feeling between two limitations

shapes the proportions

a bison frieze incessant ant-like entablature

movable types & a country for a cheapened form the inventor entirely separate & distinct from withheld information

models adopt wood a craft entirely proved two-edged the best library in england regretted by one person

the books own time to argument & to individual vaseline

type forms similar to the written letter indistinguishable from manuscript or superior to times shaped for easy expense of legibility readers renders metal worker type forms manuscripts were fit matrices manuscripts to draw the letter differing in means only conceive forms of executed exegesis a knowledge of facts recast from economic forms

achieve results of the man in the street

a degree of taste it requires they did not forget formalized legibility

this quality of legibility is difficult to explain

(& not generally understood since facts are not always type)

calcite gours 9

summer triangle

four southern regions

rocks leave their own images levels allow left & left & the & the mad dash *em* or a single feather

birdman points to one grotto

up is hard down is easier chronically horse

a laugh unabashedly wishing several flights up for relief

ability to claim space timing the constellations the sun

map constellations the bird-stick meridian columns with both feet enter the building reclaim friendship strong shorter length surprise on street lost scarf late

struggle with various vertebrae map cosmology

shapes & feathers

calcite gours 10

read the writing on the wall: the caves of lascaux cast with wax

there is no difference between what a book talks about and how it was made

– deleuze & guattari: *a thousand plateaus: capitalism & schizophrenia* p.4

with wax endeavours to find a poetic in the production, a way of conflating forms of writing and publishing in such a way as to incorporate those means into the writing itself. the poems parallel the magdalenian age (bce 13,000) caves at lascaux, france, which provide the overarching structure of the book: as the poems move through the means of production, they progress physically through the architecture of the caves themselves. it is a map of (mis)reading where the surface has not only been inscribed but also fungally infected by growths. these coloured spores blotch and obscure the texts, forcing readings outside of intention – a mondmilch of mineral deposits has grown over clarity.

the caves themselves are twisted from the limestone of the french landscape, with calcite walls and floors. condensation has formed pools and gours in the calcite floors, where slowly the mineral deposits from the cave walls are leeching the paint from the walls, settling in the pools and niches in the uneven ground.

as researchers explored the separate chambers of the lascaux caves they were confronted with both a caﬆ of prehiﬆoric animals and depictions but also a chemical brew of mineral deposits and moulds long contained in a sealed environment. the engraving and painting varied in their diﬆinctness and legibility. some, especially those in the hall of the bulls and the axial gallery, were vivid and clear, a prehiﬆoric beﬆiary carved and painted to incorporate the relief of the walls themselves. the passageways and liminal spaces between chambers were a palimpseﬆ of faint and overwritten images, literally thousands of half-formed horses, ibex, aurochs, bison, coupled with marks interpreted as aﬆrological maps, lunar charts and possible religious or societal marks; an engraved sketchpad of ideas, half-images.

these texts, like the walls of lascaux, are blotched and infected with a palimpseﬆ of hiﬆory and the process of printing; inked fingers have worked and reworked the ink, leaving scratches and burrs of meaning gathering in gours. the text is carved into the walls and leeched into our water.

acknowledgements

with wax is much indebted to neil hennessy, the best editor, closest reader & most dedicated correspondent i could hope for.

the 'calcite gours' series began as part of an eightieth birthday celebration for bob cobbing & is dedicated to his memory. thanks to catelli® for their low-fat sodium-free alphabets.

earlier versions & portions of this text appeared in *arthole, endnote, existere, olive, (orange), queen street quarterly, sudden, unarmed, van, west coast line* & *whitewall of sound* magazines; online through arras, deluxe rubber chicken, greenboathouse books, phu & lexiconjury; & in small-press editions from bellowsinwheels press, bookthug, garage, housepress, off-cut press & slowdownpress.

thanks & appreciation to glen bodner, christian bök, kyle buckley, stephen cain, jason christie, the editorial collectives of *filling station* and *dandelion* magazines, jay gamble, aaron grach, jill hartman, paul kennett, ryan knighton, larissa lai, jason le heup, kathy macpherson, angel: a raw lynx, r rickey, nikki sheppy, nathalie stephens, andrea strudensky, fred wah, darren wershler-henry & erin wood bodner, & to stan bevington, nicky drumbolis, jason mcbride, jay millar, rick/simon, alana wilcox & everyone at the coach house. & thank you, courtney.

about the author

derek beaulieu lives in calgary where he has been involved in editing the magazines *dandelion*, *filling station* and *endnote*. he is the editor/publisher of housepress, a micropress dedicated to radical poetries and poetics. his work has appeared in the *queen street quarterly*, *the capilano review* and *west coast line*.

Typeset in Adobe Caslon
Printed and bound at the Coach House
on bpNichol Lane, 2003

Edited and designed by Jay MillAr
Copy edited by Alana Wilcox
Cover image by Nikki Sheppy

Twenty-six copies of this edition,
lettered A-Z, are hand treated and signed
by the author.

Coach House Books
401 Huron Street (rear) on bpNichol Lane
Toronto Ontario
M5S 2G5

416 979 2217
1 800 367 6360

mail@chbooks.com
www.chbooks.com